Y
F
ALD
R1

Reader 1   942313
Alden, Laura
      Owl's adventure in
Alphabet Town.

Discard

DATE DUE

SE 2 6 '9			
DE 1 2 '9			
MR 1 8 '9			
JE 2 9 '95			
JY 1 5 '95			
JY 2 1 '95			

Owl's *Adventure*
in Alphabet Town

by Laura Alden
illustrated by Jodie McCallum

created by Wing Park Publishers

CHILDRENS PRESS ®
CHICAGO

Library of Congress Cataloging-in-Publication Data

Alden, Laura, 1955-
   Owl's adventure in Alphabet Town / by Laura Alden ;
illustrated by Jodie McCallum.
      p.   cm. — (Read around Alphabet Town)
   Summary: Owl meets "o" words on his adventures in
Alphabet Town. Includes activities.
   ISBN 0-516-05415-5
   [1. Owls—Fiction.   2. Alphabet—Fiction.]   I. McCallum, Jodie,
ill.   II. Title.   III. Series.
PZ7.A3586Ow   1992
[E]—dc 20   92-4091
                                                    CIP
                                                    AC

Owl's *Adventure*
in Alphabet Town

You are now entering Alphabet Town,
With houses from "A" to "Z."
I'm going on an "O" adventure today,
So come along with me.

This is the "O" house of Alphabet
Town. Owl lives here.

Owl likes everything that begins
with the letter "o."

Each day for breakfast, he has

oatmeal

and orange juice.

Then he goes outside to sit in
a big oak tree.

But one day, Owl was bored. "I do the same old thing every day," he said. "What can I do that is new?

"I know. I will ask my friends to help me. We will put on an opera. I love operas."

First Owl went to see

Ostrich.

"Will you help me put on an opera?"
he asked.

"Oh, boy," said Ostrich. "I have always wanted to sing in an opera. And I will bring Opossum to help."

Next, Owl called on

Octopus.

"Will you help me put on an opera?"
he asked.

"Okay," said Octopus. "I will play
my oboes."

Then Owl went to see

Orangutan.

"Will you help me put on an opera?"
he asked.

"Oh, yes," said Orangutan. "I will blow, 'Oompah, Oompah' on my tuba."

Owl told his friends to meet him in
the orchard. On the way there, Owl
thought of a name for them.

"Owl's One and Only Opera Company!"
he said out loud.

When the animals were all at the
orchard, Owl gave each of them a
box. "Open them," he said.

"Our opera outfits!" they cried. They put them on right away.

"And now we can begin," said Owl.
Ostrich and Opossum got ready to sing.

Octopus picked up her oboes.
Orangutan took a deep breath.

Owl lifted his wings, and the opera
began.

"Oh! Ah!" sang Ostrich and Opossum.
"Ooo! Woo!" played Octopus.
"Oompah! Oompah!" blew Orangutan.

"Ouch!" cried Owl. "This opera is hurting my ears. The show is over. This was a bad idea."

"What will we do now?" asked Opossum.
Owl had an idea. "Take off your
outfits and come with me," he said.

They all went to Owl's house.
There they ate oatmeal cookies
warm from the oven.

And Owl's One and Only Opera Company listened to opera music on the radio.

MORE FUN WITH OWL

What's in a Name?

In my "o" adventure, you read
many "o" words. My name
begins with an "O." Many of my
friends' names begin with "O"
too. Here are a few.

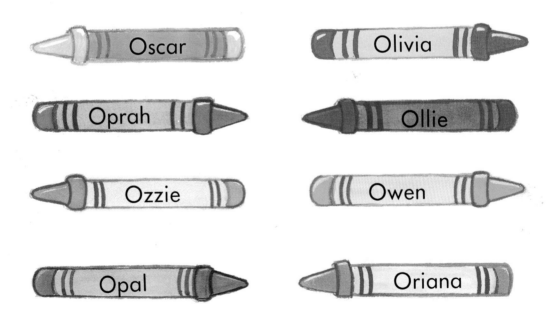

Oscar

Olivia

Oprah

Ollie

Ozzie

Owen

Opal

Oriana

Do you know other names that start with "O"?
Does your name start with "O"?

Owl's Word Hunt

I like to hunt for "o" words.
Can you help me find the words
on this page that begin with
"o"? How many are there?
Can you read them?

overalls

boat

omelet

ball

dog

radio

piano

Can you find any words with "o" in the middle?
Can you find any with "o" at the end?
Can you find a word with no "o"?

Owl's Favorite Things

"O" is my favorite letter. I love "o" things. Can you guess why? You can find some of my favorite "o" things in my house on page 7. How many "o" things can you find there? Can you think of more "o" things?

Now you make up an "o" adventure.